For the Love of Christ

A BOOK OF POETRY

Nyree Nance

Copyright © 2020 by Nyree Nance

All rights reserved. No part of this book may be used or reproduced by any means, graphic, electronic, or mechanical, including photocopying, recording, taping, or by any information storage retrieval system, without the written permission of the publisher except in the case of brief quotations embodied in critical articles and reviews.

FOR THE LOVE OF CHRIST

I, honestly, don't know where to start. My whole life I've told myself that I never wanted to write a book. I'm way too particular to complete anything, and there is nothing in my life worth writing about anyway. Yet, here I am: writing in anguish. I just want to get this over with, get it out of my system, so here we go.

How did this book come about? Funny story.

***

I was tired of crying. Every single night I would cry for what seemed like hours, for no reason at all. Then, slowly, no reason became every reason; none of which I could decipher. I was miserable, inconsolable and depressed, and I didn't even know why. I tried pinning it on my, at the time recent, "bad break-up". In actuality, it wasn't all that bad. It was definitely well overdue and greatly beneficial for all parties involved. Yet, I still found myself in an extremely dark place, mentally. I'd become someone I'd only read about; a girl who couldn't get over that one guy everyone told her she shouldn't have been with in the first place (People don't seem to realize the whole "you can do *so* much better" comment makes no sense while you're in the situation they're saying you can do better than). Nothing outside of that relationship, and us being together, made any sense to me. Especially, since after the break-up I despised my life even more than I did while we were together.

For a period, of a solid three months, I couldn't bare to get out of bed. I had no solace at home, living in what felt like a dungeon: everything seemingly grim, bitter and forsaken. I couldn't stand to be there yet, wasn't at all suitable to face the outside world. Work became a living hell. I am still convinced, to this day, my co-workers were little demons, dispatched to tear up and agonize every minute of my 8-

hour workday. I'd even begun to resent my best friend because she'd been fortunate enough to had never tasted love and had no cognizance of my affliction.

Knowing what I know now, the "break-up" had everything to do with my break-down. Although, it was inevitable and very much necessary, the separation triggered chronic anxiety. My existence, as I'd previously known it, was over. My perfectly-dreamt-up-well-thought-out-future had been obliterated. My love life, at least what I'd known it to be, was now a thing of the past.

From then on, I sought distractions and, ultimately, reverted back to partying every weekend. This went on for several months. Friday through Sunday, I'd committed to "unintentionally" attempting to kill myself. On several occasions, I got pretty darn close too. Most of my time and money wasted on recreational drugs and alcohol. Nights when I wasn't out destroying myself, I would sit in my room and sulk about how terrible my life was; crying myself to sleep every night until…one day, something happened. Right in the midst of my self-destruction…I met a guy. Yes, another one.

I don't know the science behind where love stems from. I have my theories. I do know that it's a beautiful burst of every good thing, and when it is done right it has the power to change any person and/or outcome of any situation. The problem is *getting it right*. Sometimes the way we are taught to love, isn't really love at all! This book is about deciphering between illusions of love versus what is true. That is, of course, the true and perfect love of Jesus Christ. If we could only learn to follow His lead and to love as He loves us, this world would be a miraculous place. One could only hope…

FOR THE LOVE OF CHRIST

"Love is patient, love is kind. It does not envy, it does not boast, it is not proud. It does not dishonor others, it is not self-seeking, it is not easily angered, it keeps no record of wrongs. Love does not delight in evil but rejoice with the truth. It always protects, always trusts, always hopes, always perseveres. Love never fails..."

(1 Corinthians 13:4-8, NIV)

FOR THE LOVE OF CHRIST

A Run On

False realities better known as illusions often characterized by abuse and misuse cause us to want to escape to a relatable place with those around us whom are searching every day but there is no other way except to die every day and awake to find the beauty of a new day not promised but given solely by grace I am amazed so amazed by how long it takes to realize the compass we've been given to get out of this maze. Love.

To be continued...

FOR THE LOVE OF CHRIST

Serial Dater

You deserve to stay on your toes
So, I keep you there
Hold your breath
Long enough for me to steal it
You had every intention to sweep me
I only hope that you keep me
Bold enough to reveal your soul
Yet vulnerable for me to
Break. You.
I think we'll do just fine
Plans for getaways across nations
Open oceans and lost seas
I don't care how far we go
Just as long as you're near
Nope!
I never do this
Never lost my mind behind
A strong
Intelligent
Beautiful
Black
Well, never mind
The only fact that matters is
This
& We

FOR THE LOVE OF CHRIST

& Us
It's Forever
Not like the last time
Nooo...I mean
Forever like
Ever
Just me
&
All of you

FOR THE LOVE OF CHRIST

A Wretch Like Me

I gave no thought to expectations
Only reservations
And thought for a moment
I could escape you
It turns out that
You were not only my destiny
You created it

You created it and everything in it
I owe You gratitude
Gratitude that could never afford
The debt You paid
A ransom
For a castaway

Thank you

Thank You for seeing
Past my flaws
At least that's what You said

You and I both know
There is no getting around the skin
I'm in
Every scar You kissed them

FOR THE LOVE OF CHRIST

And released the prison
That kept me bound for so long
Blind without opportunity
To see again

The world I lived in
Had no knowledge of You

If it wasn't for Your life
Your death and
Deliverance
I would still be oblivious

So I guess what I'm
Trying to say is
Your grace
Is
Amazing

Vain Oblations

I clipped my wings for you.
I knew it wasn't in you to soar so,
I made myself okay with
The fact that
I, like you, would be grounded for life
I made myself forget what the blue sky looked like
as I held your hand along the way
Whenever I had the nerve to remember
I would look at your smile and forget
I ever had dreams of flying
I got used to walking,
sometimes I even ran, and that was fun.
I gave you the noose to pull
just in case I strayed too far
I never went too far though,
I wouldn't dare leave you
Though times I became curious
They were always brief
Other times I'd have weird feelings
As If...
I was missing something
Everything, a life
Far away from you.
Then that feeling would vanish,
& I'd become content again

FOR THE LOVE OF CHRIST

Accepting my reality
It is liberating
Knowing I gave up my dreams for love
You taught me to accept normalcy,
I Thank you.
I realize there isn't much to life without you
& at this rate, I'll never know.
You've shown me how to be content
The blue skies now seem like a figment
I used to be so close to them,
Funny I assumed them my destiny before
What a shame.
Good thing I found you,
There's no telling where I'd be
If you'd never clipped my wings.

FOR THE LOVE OF CHRIST

Clipped Wings

Thank You God for clipping my wings
There's no telling where them old things
Would have taken me
Just look at where I've already been
Dwelling in caves, gross places
My light has grown dim
I used to admire those old things,
Those wings
Look at them & be proud
of where they had taken me
I admit, I let them consume me
Every now & again
I would take flight & get high
Soar high enough
Until I could forget how lonely I was
In the clouds
Thinking but not really thinking
"This is it"
Not even knowing there was
Something else up there
All I could see was those old things,
Those wings
I Thank You,
Lord for delivering me

FOR THE LOVE OF CHRIST

Lit

The fire in your eyes is magnetic.
I admit, it's…hypnotizing.

Too bad it's misdirected
& misguided
The direction that you're headed
I would never be able to follow

I am trying to merit a
Resurrection

I can say it's tempting.
But

Temptation is not
Strong enough to
Knock me off my
High horse

I'm in full force
To my promise

I've decided to stay
On my course

FOR THE LOVE OF CHRIST

To be honest
It's nothing I haven't
Seen before

You know

That kindle
That's got you set ablaze
Giving the Son a run for
His money
Just to get you saved

Problem is your energy
is limited
Lost

Like a mouse in a maze
I'm hoping
For your sake
It's just a phase

The least I can do is
Pray

Salvation will get ahold of
You
One day

FOR THE LOVE OF CHRIST

Tick Tock

I'll wait all day
For your grace to bless
My presence
I was and will always be
Nothing without you
Therefore
I wait
I wait
To tell You thanks
For Your life
That You gave
Just for mine
I'd tell you
That I wasn't worth
That much
But I can't stand
The possibility of
Ever being without you
Again
This love takes me
Beyond seas
Above rainbows
And there's still so
Much more
So much more

FOR THE LOVE OF CHRIST

That my mind cannot
Grasp
The way you love me
I'll never understand
All I can do
Is try
To walk worthy
Of being called by Your name
To say that I know You
Please don't be ashamed
You gave Your life
For mine
The least I can do
Is wait for You
To come in
Just so I can say
Thank You

FOR THE LOVE OF CHRIST

Breath Taking

My breath left my body.
I was reminded why I'd stayed so far away.
For so long.
I could see myself sitting there.
As my mind went far far away.
The voices are now muffled,
But continue without hesitation.
"...marry me" rings loud and clear
On repeat
I can't figure why I can't gather my feet.
I would like to be able to run away from here
Just like I've always done
Run far away and pretend this...
Nothing like this...Had ever happened
Instead, I sit across from a man
A man that loves her
I wonder if he even knows her
I answer that one on my own
He can't.
Or else I wouldn't be here.
I wouldn't be sitting across from him
& he wouldn't be asking ME,
Me, of all people
What she would want.
He would know that it isn't him.

FOR THE LOVE OF CHRIST

That is, if he knew her.

He wants to marry MY girl.
He's grinning, and
I wonder if He can read my thoughts.
Has this been a game all along?
Can he see the tears I fight from falling?
Rugged breathing cause my breast to rise and fall
Without any constraint
Reminding me of my womanhood
I could never be a husband to her.
All of a sudden the laughs don't matter
The late nights we'd stayed up sharing secrets
They don't matter
I want to be angry with her for leading me here
But she only held out her hand
And I was so ready
So willing
My heart is filled with anguish
Knowing that I was only a friend
A friend who turned into a casual lover
When she,
She was my everything.
Now, it's over.

Alternative Lifestyle

I thought I had lost my way
When she left, but truly
I had never known The Way
All I'd ever known, was this way
& apparently I'd been wrong all along
& now that I'm alone
I realize, it's time for redirection,
Correction.
No more, empty "love" & false affection
I need The Truth, The Way,
The Life
The Light
& In spite of
how I feel, something is telling me
That You are real!
Because when I was falling
Waiting to collide with the ground
It was You I found
So precious & holy, so ready to hold me
Almost as if You'd been waiting on me
I didn't believe in you, but
You reached out to mold me,
Really got to know me
& by doing so, You've shown me
That You believe in me

FOR THE LOVE OF CHRIST

Porcelain

How long do I have to smile?
I sit with my legs crossed neatly
my fingers intertwined
avidly pretend I'm enjoying my wine
While you entertain
And I smile on cue
I'm really a vodka girl
But I gave that up years ago...
along with several other things I once loved
I'm still trying to remember exactly
When I gave up my right to live
I can't even say I got anything out of this
A nice purse maybe,
Only to be glorified for my shininess and newness
I have no real use
At least, that's what you tell me
No use to you anyway
Except for...you know when
And thank God for Glenn, our Cook
Talented & Multi-Purposed
I've learned
Less mess I have to clean up
It just sucks because in the End
I'm the one
Stuck

Pretending

I Let My Guard Down.
So you can see my flaws clearly,
You see right through me
& somehow I'm okay with this
I know that I cannot hide
And maybe that's why
Today,
I choose to let go
Of my pride
No one else can know
What I hide inside
It's an ugly truth, where
Terror & turmoil resides
Yet, you know how to settle
All these things
& you don't run
Nor deny me
As being one of Your own
Sometimes, I can't smile
With You,
I don't have to pretend
I love You for being
More than a friend.

Restless Waters

I want to wrap my arms around you
Although, I know what it will do to me
I'll forget everything you said
Your warmth will melt
Every bit of any resentment
And shape it into small Beautiful things
Butterflies with colorful wings
The doubt I once held Strong and Bold
Will be replaced with Forgiveness & Hope
I lay still,
Until my hands move before me
Beyond my control
They constantly betray me in this relationship
As you've always been,
Too much to hold
Yet, you say you belong to me
And though, at times, I'm displeased
With your nature
I convince myself, that you are mine.
My fingertips
Graze your skin
& the waves begin
I let them consume me
It's easier than fighting them
After all, they are so strong

FOR THE LOVE OF CHRIST

& they run so deep.
Going from raging to Calm again
I give in.
Closing my eyes
Once again.
I pray for the peace

FOR THE LOVE OF CHRIST

Your Love Is Never Ending

The only thing that can awaken this dead being
Who am I to deserve such a thing?
Such a beautiful thing
You give me each day
Holding me in your arms
You whisper "Everything's okay"
Never do I need to worry
I never even have a care
As long as my eyes are open
(even when they are not),
I know you are there
I can't explain how I feel
I can hardly contain my gladness
Only your hand can wipe away my sadness
I want to call it love,
but I can't
Knowing that it can never be
As perfect as the way you love me
How can you be so Faithful?
How can you be so True?
Without any explanation
I'm still grateful for You

Face Time

"It was good to see you."

A phrase I said ever so often
Hardly without meaning
A formality that is
Often mistaken for
Sincerity

I did miss the longing
In his eyes
They told more stories
Than his lips had
Time to utter
Confirmed that
He missed the girl
I used to be
And was dying to see
If she was buried beneath
This new found beauty
Of unfamiliarity

I smirked wholeheartedly
Uneasily
Knowing the reflection
He gave was full

FOR THE LOVE OF CHRIST

of uncertainty
The inability to
Please me

I could feel the pain
Increase
Once buried deep
And unseen
Was rising to the
Tippy tip part
Of my neck
Forming a lump
As I gazed into
His naked soul
Filled with stories
Untold
I longed to know
What he longed to
Share
Memories he
Created
With others
Had he'd wished I'd been there

As quickly as he
Came
He was gone again
A crude joke

FOR THE LOVE OF CHRIST

Filled the silence
Reminding us
Of the years between
Us
A little time
A lot of wisdom
Would never bring
Us together again

Life learned to pull
Us in different directions
Found on different ends
Of the spectrum
Both playing our part
In society not
Wiling to come down

We wave goodbye
With a broken promise
Almost as broken as our
Love
To call back
When he got a chance
A lie we'd both learned
To live with
Because in between
Forgiveness and a
Decision that cost

FOR THE LOVE OF CHRIST

Me my life
He found his world
Without me
While I found
Christ

FOR THE LOVE OF CHRIST

A Perfect Love

I'm glad His love is not like mine
I admit, I forget who I am sometime
I can't distinguish your faults from you
Mistakes are all that I know of you
But God's love is greater
So much greater

I know, to survive, I must strive
To be more like Him everyday
He has shown me the way to live
In peace
Not just for now, but Forever!
He loves me so much
That it overflows and you see,
Now I have enough left over to love you...
As He intended

Seasons

The glimmer in your eyes
I hardly recognize
Your smile, although beautiful,
is unfamiliar to me
Once resounding,
it has diminished over time and
I don't blame it
What reason have I given you to smile?
I'm not who I once was
The same jovial girl whose laughter
Was once your weakness
It's okay.
Tell me
I beg you, but you don't hear me
You do, but you ignore me
I lay my pride before me
Struggling to restore me
I just can't think of one reason to smile.

FOR THE LOVE OF CHRIST

The Tears Burn

They're fast and deliberate.
They come down one at a time
Each containing one specific detail
That contributes to the rotting of my soul
Okay, maybe not that extreme.
When I'm done,
I'd bet I'll still have my soul
It'll just be a little different
A couple of shades darker, maybe.
I imagine one day it'll be close to Black,
But at least I'll still have my soul.
It's my heart though, that I worry about.
I'm not sure how much more
That poor thing can take
Heartbreak after heartbreak
I can feel it chipping away.
I wonder how much of it is left.
I sort of wish it would just be done.
I've experienced this before.
It never gets any easier,
That's why the tears come.
And the tears?
They burn.

Intimacy

I cried until I had no more tears
Sought until I had no more fears
You showed Your face to me
And I forgot all the years...
That I'd never known You

Peace restored
In a place it's never been
The ways of this world
Blow as strong as the wind
They seek to destroy me
But You live within

Your peace is enough
To calm the trees
Your armor declares the victory
The roaring winds stifled
To merely a breeze

All because I know You

FOR THE LOVE OF CHRIST

Hangman

Feet 6inches from the edge
Fingers slipping
Grip loosening
I don't have fear in me
Nope
Teeth crushing one another
Bottom against top
The pain is severe
But I'm numb to it
The disappointment
Has me ready
To be done with it
There is therefore
Now
No condemnation
To them which are in
Christ Jesus
What about those who want to be
But simply cannot
Walk after the spirit
Sounds light and attainable
But it's not
Do I condemn myself now
Or Later
Because the greater

FOR THE LOVE OF CHRIST

That says He's within me
Is feeling very very
Small right now
Arms trembling
I'm just ready
To. Let. Go.
What's the point of holding on
You say You love me
Yet
I feel so alone
So
Alone
On this rope
Ready to give it all up
For one night
One love
One single touch
That lead to destruction

FOR THE LOVE OF CHRIST

Two Angels

I climbed without looking back
I didn't look down or anything
I made up my mind
That up there was where
I wanted
I needed
To be

I was leaving everything
Behind me
I didn't want
Any traces of
Where I'd gone

That's the reason
I left in the middle
of the night
Without a note

I doubt anyone would
Miss me anyway
So, I climbed
Higher

The end

FOR THE LOVE OF CHRIST

Came nearer
I assumed fear
Would make me
Turn around
But it's too late now

I looked around
At the beginning
Of the end
I'm ready to
End
I look out
At what I'm
Now free from
A humming
Unsettling stir

Not exactly what
I was expecting
But I lean
Anyway

Over the edge
I tell myself
It's okay
I pray
With my final
Breath

FOR THE LOVE OF CHRIST

And let all
The stress
Fall freely
Off of me
As I freely
Fall

The wind fights me
But it can't stop me
I told you
I made up my mind
I'm free

When something
Someone grabbed me
I open my eyes
To try and see
But the wind is
Blowing
Vehemently

The only thing
I'm able to make out
Is a hand
Two to be exact

One on my right

FOR THE LOVE OF CHRIST

And
One on my left

All of a sudden
The winds stop
Blowing

My arms are
Being held up
By something
Someone

And before I know it
I'm back on my
Feet
The two hands
I once seen
Have departed from me

I'm alone
Or so, I think
I look around
And nothing
Surrounds me

But peace

But God

FOR THE LOVE OF CHRIST

I know
Without a
Shadow of a
Doubt

It was Him
He saved me

Perfect Timing

Drops of blood led me to you
They are the very reason
Nothing will ever separate us

I am in awe of your mercy
The mercy that wasn't given
You now freely give
My heart aches under the
Weight of your grace
Overwhelmed with the love
That you have
For a wretched
Soul that is me
Arms outstretched
You called us home
As you went on
To be with Your Father
Hands opened wide
You accepted my flaws
Sin and all
As Your own
Now I am
Yours

FOR THE LOVE OF CHRIST

A Sorry Sorry

As I apologize one more time
I know you've heard it all before
It's at least worth a try
I see that look in your eyes
Disappointment and disbelief
That I could fail you once again
I am dismayed that I allowed this
To fall upon you
But who am I
Just another being void of love
Refusing to acknowledge my help
I wait for your acceptance
Of my broken down
Not near authentic
Strained apology.
Your silence is so long
I cry inside
Knowing that this could
Very well be
The last time.
I imagine you contemplating
The extreme of my offense

Am I worth forgiving?

FOR THE LOVE OF CHRIST

Grace

Drips from the sky like
Rainbow Rays
Never judging
Only loving
Without reserve
Undeservingly

Following me
With motive
Covering me
With Warmth
It's Necessary
for my survival

Every now
And again
And again
I slip and fall
From underneath
The shadow of
Love
And grace
Slows down
Stops and picks
Me up

FOR THE LOVE OF CHRIST

Coupled with
Mercy
You can say
I am blessed
Aimlessly strutting
An ignorant mess

Grace falls from
The sky like
He knows my name
When God sent
His Love
Beautifully
Wrapped in Grace

Blurred Lines

I can't remember the last time
I've seen the lines in my hands

I look and stare in amazement
At the beauty of being free

Everything I've been holding onto
Has been loosed from me

I give it all to You as a gift
All of which You accept gladly

& let a welcoming peace fall upon me
I shiver at the mystery of the unknown

Oh my! How I've grown!
I hereby pronounce that I renounce

Being on my own
I give up that control

And choose today, to be free
To take up my cross daily,

FOR THE LOVE OF CHRIST

*To follow Thee
Unto the everlasting
Peace of salvation*

www.ingramcontent.com/pod-product-compliance
Lightning Source LLC
Chambersburg PA
CBHW070858050426
42453CB00012B/2264